SALVATION

in

SPIRIT

SOUL

and

BODY

Paul & Nuala O'Higgins

"Salvation Of Spirit, Soul & Body
by Paul & Nuala O'Higgins
Published By Reconciliation Outreach
© All rights reserved
First Edition 2015

TABLE OF CONTENTS

INTRODUCTION	4
I THE NEW COVENANT	11
II RELEASE FROM SIN'S PENALTY	18
III RELEASE FROM SIN'S POWER	25
IV RELEASE FROM THE WORLD	33
V SPIRIT, SOUL & BODY	45

INTRODUCTION

The work of Jesus for us is the most wonderful event in human history. It is also the most significant.

His work releases us from
- THE PENALTY OF SIN
- THE POWER OF SIN &
- THE WORLD'S AGENDA.

Countless people struggle with issues of shame and guilt. They wonder about the meaning and significance of their existence. Within their hearts there is a longing for greater significance, yet they feel entrapped in cycles of emptiness and despair. They struggle with problems arising from greed, covetousness, insecurity, sexual disorders, alcoholism and drug addiction etc. These dysfunctional behaviors are the cause of much of the personal and social misery in the world today.

Jesus offers a solution to all of these problems: the issue of guilt, the issue of identity and destiny in life and eternity, and the issue of liberation from bondage to dysfunctional and self-destructive behaviors. His sublime moral teaching, His atoning sacrifice and His work of bearing the sin, guilt and curse of our sins has changed the world. The task of communicating the facts of what He accomplished for us by His death, resurrection and ascension has been commissioned to the entire Body of Christ.

In these days of restoration and recovery the Holy Spirit is clarifying what the gospel is: the proclamation of what exactly Jesus did for us on the Cross, how we can put our faith in it and so live in the Spirit.

For centuries there has been controversy and division between
- those who point to the acceptance we receive from God when we believe from the heart THE FACT that Jesus has fully paid for our sins
- and those who say that our salvation can only be maintained by holy and upright living.

Both camps (the Calvinist and the Arminian - as the theologians call them) have talked passed each other, creating more heat than light. One group emphasizes release from the *penalty* of sins (while ignoring the release from the *power* of sin) and the others make the release from the *power* of sin the condition of being released from the *penalty* of sin.

It is time for the truth that both groups embrace to be rightly understood (each in its own context) so that the Body of Christ proclaims not only release from THE PENALTY OF SIN but also release from THE POWER OF SIN. This can be done without diluting the assurance of salvation that is ours through faith or diluting the responsibility and privilege we have to reflect the character and nature of Christ, by the power of the Holy Spirit.

Many forget that Jesus also invites us to follow Him into *a third level of salvation* - salvation from the control of the world. He sends us into the world to be in it but not of it i.e. to be in it but not directed by its values.

"My prayer is not that you take them out of the world but that you protect them from the evil one." (John 17:15)

Jesus liberates all who follow Him from the agenda of ego, ambition, and the agenda of this world. He calls us from conformity to the values presented by the world systems to a life of love and service. He calls us to a new agenda for our lives: to participate with Him in bringing His love, mercy and ways to the world. *"Follow me and I will make you become fishers of men"* (Matt. 4:19)

In this book we shall see that we are saved from the PENALTY of sin by faith in the Atoning Sacrifice of Jesus and from the POWER of sin by receiving and yielding to the life of the Spirit. We also explore a third level of freedom which God has provided for us through the gospel: freedom from the dominion and agenda of the world i.e. freedom FROM THE CONTROLLING SYSTEMS OF THIS AGE.

For the believer to come to the fullness of his destiny in Christ he must know

- Freedom from the penalty of sin
- Freedom from the power of sin and
- Freedom from the agenda of the world.

The purpose of God in Christ is to save us from our sins and to implant the divine nature in us. Jesus was sent to lift us out of the "miry pit" of sin, guilt and immoral living, and to implant His nature in us so that we could live as sons of God. The heart of God is to see mankind restored to His image and likeness to reproduce the wisdom, righteousness, compassion and dignity of His nature in us.

By focusing only on the release from sins penalty the Calvinist camp often neglect the importance of living upright lives in the power of the Spirit. By focusing on performance as a means of maintaining salvation the Arminians rob believers of the security that belongs to those who are accepted fully not on the basis of our performance, but on what Jesus did *for* us.

The fact that *acceptance* is not on the basis of performance does not mean that performance does not matter. To fail to live the New Life Christ empowers us for will cause us to miss many aspects of our inheritance in the Kingdom of God. Jesus has done enough on the Cross. By implying we are no longer acceptable if our *performance* falls short causes many to react in despair believing the Christian life is an unattainable goal.

The confusion arises from the fact the we have failed to distinguish between SPIRIT, SOUL & BODY and to recognize the difference between the salvation of the spirit, the salvation of the soul and the salvation of the body.

Furthermore we have failed to distinguish between going to Heaven when we die and entering into the Kingdom of God here on earth. We can enter the Kingdom of God on earth by living a life under the Lordship of Jesus in the power of the Spirit. There is a clear difference between going to Heaven when we die and living in the Kingdom of God here on earth

Not all who are 'saved' i.e. who have accepted Jesus as Savior and received forgiveness of sin on the basis of faith in the Atoning Sacrifice go on to live a life of obedience in the power of the Spirit. To be born again assures us of entrance into Heaven when we die. But Jesus also tells us that when we are born again we SEE the Kingdom of God. He tells us in His teachings many things we need to do i.e. many ways we are to cooperate with God to ENTER the kingdom of God.

An immigrant can be given citizen papers to his new country by an act of a government official. There is a difference between the possession of citizen papers and living a productive life in the new county. Faith in Jesus assures of us of our citizen papers to Heaven but it is quite another matter to enter the life and lifestyle of the Kingdom of Heaven and to *walk* in the ways of the Lord by the power of His Spirit.

Some are so focused on the citizen papers for Heaven that they neglect to challenge believers to walk in the lifestyle of the Kingdom of God. Others so focus on their new responsibilities that they forget that their citizenship papers for Heaven are assured on the basis of faith in the Cross of Jesus, and not on performance or earning 'brownie points.'

Chapter I

THE NEW COVENANT

The Ten Commandments and the religious laws that were given to Moses for the Children of Israel on Mount Sinai exposed man's sinfulness and the evil that is in his heart. If there was no moral law we would not be aware of the sinfulness of our actions and would - like many people today - assume that sin and lawless behavior are normal. God however reveals that any kind of immorality, especially idolatry, sexual immorality, envy, covetousness and hatred is evil and estranges us from His presence.

The source of this evil, which is in us like a cancer, goes back to the earliest days of mankind's existence. Our ancestors (Adam & Eve) chose to disconnect themselves from dependence and intimate relationship with God, their Creator and life giver. They did not deny His existence but simply chose to live independently from His advice and help. They chose to know "good and evil" for themselves apart from God's counsel. That is what the scriptures mean when they tell us that Adam and Eve ate of the 'Tree of the Knowledge of Good & Evil'. They believed the lie of Satan that if they ate of this tree they would be 'as God' knowing good and evil apart from God. They became *independent* and removed themselves from *dependence*. As a result their spirits (and those of all their descendants) became disconnected from God. Faith in Jesus' Cross restores the connection. God, Our Loving Heavenly Father, made us to remain dependent on Him. He wants us to renounce independence so that He can continually guide and help us.

Pride towards God is the attitude of anyone who refuses His help. God cannot help those who refuse His help. In refusing His help and going our own way we also fell under the dominion of satanic powers which oppress and blind us. The present condition of mankind is far short of what He intended for us. His plan has always been for us to live in the atmosphere of His love, under the shelter of His protections, receiving His help, care, guidance, support and His blessing on all we do.

The Sinai Covenant reveals the mercy and compassion of God for mankind even in His sinful state and provided the Jewish people not only with moral standards but also with a system of Atonement. Whenever they sinned - violated God's laws - they could be temporarily restored to fellowship with God by repentance and bringing to God the sacrifice that He prescribed and provided. (Leviticus 16:22)

The Sinai Covenant however, provided no *permanent* cure for the problem of our estrangement from God's presence and no permanent cure for the wickedness in man's hearts. It was like a hospital with a diagnostic and radiology department but with no surgery and medical department. It provided the diagnosis but not the cure. The Prophets saw the inadequacy and insufficiency of the Sinai Covenant.

God told them that He was going to make a New Covenant that would provide *permanent atonement* for sin and clean *mankind's heart* from the inside. The Lord promised to remove wickedness from our hearts and replace the wicked side of our nature with His own nature by putting His Spirit within us.

"Surely he has borne our griefs and carried our sorrows; yet we esteemed him stricken, smitten by God, and afflicted. But he was pierced for our transgressions; he was crushed for our iniquities; the chastisement that brought us peace was upon him and with his wounds we are healed. All we like sheep have gone astray; we have turned - every one - to his own way; and the Lord has laid on him the iniquity of us all" (Isaiah 53:4-6)

This describes the details of Jesus' crucifixion nearly 600 years before it happened. The prophets foretold the work of the Messiah *before it happened.* The gospels describe the work of the Messiah Jesus *as it happened* and the letters of Paul, James, John and Peter describe *what was accomplished* by the death resurrection and ascension of Jesus.

"And I will give you a new heart, and I will put a new spirit in you. I will take out your stony, stubborn heart and give you a tender, responsive heart. And I will put my Spirit in you so that you will follow my decrees and be careful to obey my regulations." (Ezekiel 36:26-27)

"The day is coming," says the Lord, "when I will make a new covenant with the people of Israel and Judah. This covenant will not be like the one I made with their ancestors when I took them by the hand and brought them out of the land of Egypt. They broke that covenant, though I loved them as a husband loves his wife," says the Lord.

"But this is the new covenant I will make with the people of Israel after those days," says the Lord. "I will put my instructions deep within them, and I will write them on their hearts. I will be their God, and they will be my people. And they will not need to teach their neighbors, nor will they need to teach their relatives, saying, 'You should know the Lord.' For everyone, from the least to the greatest, will know me already," says the Lord. "And I will forgive their wickedness, and I will never again remember their sins." (Jeremiah 31:31-34)

Permanent Atonement & A New Heart

In these three great prophecies we read that God promised to send the Messiah

- To take on Himself the guilt of all people in a once-for all event.
- To make a new covenant where the sins of believers would be remembered no more because of the Blood of Jesus.
- To clean us from the inside by removing the evil side of our nature and replacing it with His own Spirit
- To produce a people reconciled to Himself and walking in His ways.

God's plan was greater than that revealed at Sinai to Moses - the New Covenant enacted by Jesus in Jerusalem

(1) By sending His only begotten Son to bear our sin and guilt He provides PERMANENT TOTAL atonement for our sins. By this we can be permanently reconciled to Him and restored to His care.

(2) By extracting from us the evil component of our

nature and implanting His own Spirit within us, He empowers us to walk in His ways.

This is exactly what Jesus did when He came among us. He died for our sins, taught the ways of righteousness, and left His Spirit to those who received Him. He pointed out the inadequacy of the Sinai religion - or any religion - that consists merely of moral advice.

"What comes out of a person is what defiles him. For from within, out of the heart of man, come evil thoughts, sexual immorality, theft, murder, adultery, coveting, wickedness, deceit, sensuality, envy, slander, pride, foolishness. All these evil things come from within, and they defile a person." (Mark 7:20-23)

"Woe to you, scribes and Pharisees, hypocrites! For you clean the outside of the cup and the plate, but inside they are full of greed and self-indulgence." (Matt. 23:25)

Here Jesus is describing the wickedness that is in the heart of all humans (religious and non-religious alike.) God dealt with this wickedness by providing atonement and giving us a new heart - His own Spirit to live within us. Jesus became

- The bearer of our guilt and
- The provider of our righteous life.

There is more than the remission of sin. Jesus cleanses as many as believe in Him and empowers them to walk in the transcendent way of His kingdom. He does not condemn because He bears our condemnation, and He does not make harsh demands because He puts His own Spirit in us to EMPOWER us to live by His ways.

CHAPTER II

RELEASE FROM SINS' PENALTY

Let's look now at how the gospel releases us (saves us) from the penalty of sin. Under God's law at Sinai, violation of the moral Law brought a penalty of death. The guilt of sin, however, could be transferred on to a sacrificial Lamb and the Lamb would bear the guilt on behalf of the guilty party. This is illustrated by the repeated sacrifices that were offered in the Tabernacle and in the Temple and described in detail in the Book of Leviticus.

Under the Law we are all found to be short of God's perfect standard and would be liable to the death penalty. Under the stern standards of perfect morality the penalty for sin is death and it disqualifies us from entering into the Holy and perfect presence of God. Our Heavenly Father, however, seeing the guilt that we all have under the Law, did something outrageously compassionate. His extravagant love provoked Him to send His Son Jesus to assume on Himself the guilt of all our sin and failings.

The amazing fact of the Atoning Sacrifice - the death of Jesus on the Cross on our behalf - is that God transferred on to Him all the blame shame and guilt of all of us. *"The Lord has laid on Him the iniquity of us all."* (Isaiah 53:6) The iniquity and guilt of every Jew and gentile was transferred from them on to the Messiah, Jesus.

When we believe from the heart in what He has done, God transfers our unrighteousness on to Jesus and transfers His righteousness on to us!! A great transfer takes place. God transfers on to Jesus our condemnation and transfers on to us Jesus' righteousness. This is the great revolution of The Cross

"Therefore, if anyone is in Christ, he is a new creation; old things have passed away; behold, all things have become new. Now all things are of God, who has reconciled us to Himself through Jesus Christ, and has given us the ministry of reconciliation, that is, that God was in Christ reconciling the world to Himself, not imputing their trespasses to them, and has committed to us the word of reconciliation. Now then, we are ambassadors for Christ, as though God were pleading through us: we implore you on Christ's behalf, be reconciled to God. For He made Him who knew no sin to be sin for us, that we might become the righteousness of God in Him." (2 Cor. 5:17-21)

He takes our shame and gives us His right standing with God. The Righteous One steps in to bear the death penalty of the unrighteous ones. God nailed all the judgments the Law had against us on Jesus so we can now approach God on the basis of this fact and enter His presence fully forgiven and fully accepted.

No Double Jeopardy

In secular law once an offense is paid e.g. the felon has done his time in prison and been released, or paid the fine assessed by the court, he cannot be charged for that same crime again. This is the principle of 'No Double Jeopardy.'

We were all found guilty before God, but

Jesus took our legal penalty leaving us legally exonerated in the sight of God, Our Father. Since Jesus has legally borne the guilt of our sins we cannot be accused of those sins again and we are legally justified. This justification - it is a *fact* in God's eyes. It simply remains for us *to put our faith in it* and return to God accepting the reconciliation that has been provided for us by Our Heavenly Father.

God had said to Abraham *"I myself will provide a Ram"* and prevented him from offering his son, Isaac, as sacrifice to God. Our Heavenly Father made it clear that He does not need a sacrifice from us to appease His anger or to satisfy the justice system of heaven. We should never think that we need to offer God a sacrifice for our sin. Such an idea comes from paganism and is not Christian. It is God who made a sacrifice of His own Son for us to bear our guilt.

Through the death of Jesus the legal side of our guilt has been fully satisfied and the way is open for confident and bold access to His presence. God, Himself, took full responsibly for our sins so that we can be liberated and return to the grace of God with the issue of sin and guilt removed. Our heavenly Father Himself offered His Son to bear our sins and Jesus obeyed and accepted this commission.

When we put our faith in the great work of God for us we are ushered into a new dimension - the dimension of the Glory of God - which is the realm of His goodness longsuffering and continuous mercy. The love of God comes flooding into our hearts like light into a room when the curtains are pulled back and the Spirit of God infills our hearts.

"Therefore, having been justified by faith, we have peace with God through our Lord Jesus Christ, through whom also we have access by faith into this grace in which we stand, and rejoice in hope of the glory of God.. And not only that, but we also glory in tribulations, knowing. ...Now hope does not disappoint, because the love of God has been poured out in our hearts by the Holy Spirit who was given to us." (Romans 5:1,2-3, 5)

Our acceptance with God is COMPLETE. We are *"fully accepted in the beloved."* (Eph. 1:6) By grace, we are saved from the penalty of our sins and restored into fellowship with God. It is not our own achievement, it is the gift from God.

This plan that Jesus would bear our guilt - the innocent for the guilty - was settled in heaven before the foundation of the world. Jesus came to earth and enacted this plan on the Cross. His resurrection is the evidence of the fact that he successfully bore our sins and lives now to impart His life to us.

The tearing of the veil of the Temple at the hour of Jesus death (Matt. 27:51) is the symbol that we can now approach God's presence with the issue of sin and guilt removed. The gospel invites all to put their faith in this fact and be restored to the favor and blessing of God and to receive His life in our Spirit.

"Therefore, brethren, having boldness to enter the Holiest by the blood of Jesus, by a new and living way which He consecrated for us, through the veil, that is, His flesh, and having a High Priest over the house of God, let us draw near with a true heart in full assurance of faith, having our hearts sprinkled from an evil conscience and our bodies washed with

pure water." (Hebrews 10:19-22)

"In him we have redemption through his blood, the forgiveness of our trespasses, according to the riches of his grace, which he lavished upon us, in all wisdom and insight making known to us the mystery of his will, according to his purpose, which he set forth in Christ as a plan for the fullness of time, to unite all things in him, things in heaven and things on earth." (Eph. 1:7-10)

It is now possible for all men to come home, through faith and repentance to the blessing, pardon and love of God through the wonderful work of Jesus' death and blood. The gospel is the invitation to all, from every tribe and background - no matter how oppressed, disadvantaged or shameful - to be restored to God and to *"come streaming to the goodness of God."* (Jeremiah 31:12)

The blessings of Abraham who was *"blessed in all things"* (Genesis 24:1) are now, as God promised Abraham, extended to all (from every nation) who seek to be reconciled by God.

"Christ has redeemed us from the curse of the law, (i.e. the curse prescribed by the Law on all who broke it) *"having become a curse for us (for it is written, 'Cursed is everyone who hangs on a tree' that the blessing of Abraham might come upon the Gentiles in Christ Jesus, that we might receive the promise of the Spirit through faith."* (Gal. 3:13-14)

When we put our faith in what God had done for us we receive reconciliation, restoration, the blessings of Abraham and the life of the Spirit. What amazing grace!

Where religion and human effort failed to

bridge the gap between man and God - God bridged the gap Himself. It is a new and living way. This is being proclaimed and discovered by millions across the globe and they are streaming to the goodness of God on the basis of God's gift.

"By grace you have been saved through faith - not by works lest anyone should boast. It is the gift of God." (Eph. 2:8-9)

When we proclaim the gospel we show mankind what God has done for them and invite them to receive by faith the free gift of Salvation and right standing with God.

Chapter III

RELEASE FROM SIN'S POWER

We have seen that God accepts us not on the basis of our behavior but IN SPITE of it because He has laid our sins on Jesus. It is not that we were without sin or guilt - on the contrary - it is because we were full of it that God laid our sin on Jesus. None of us can boast - we are all equally in need of the gift of reconciliation. The ground is level at the foot of the Cross.

At this point some believers get a little confused and say that since we were not accepted by our behavior it does not matter how we live - we can do as we please. This ignores that the purpose of God is not only - as we have said - *to remove us* from the *penalty* and guilt of sin but also *to free us* from the *power* of Sin.

"Well then, should we keep on sinning so that God can show us more and more of his wonderful grace? Of course not! Since we have died to sin, how can we continue to live in it?" (Romans 6:1-2)

No one who seeks release from sin's penalty can take this as a license to continue in sin. Such people are not sincere in asking God to forgive them their sins. Whenever we ask anyone to forgive us we are also implicitly saying that we want to turn away from the actions and attitudes that cause the hurt and offence.

Some think that they can come to God for forgiveness of sin and not make any effort to resist sin or turn away from it. That is *license*. Others think that what God requires is that we get our sins forgiven and then try harder to live a perfect Christian life by their own will-power. That is legalism. It is in fact impossible. It would be like asking a monkey to behave like a human.

Saved By His Life

While the **blood of Jesus** saves us from **sin's penalty,** the life of Jesus (which comes to us in New Birth) saves us from **sins' power**.

"For if, while we were God's enemies, we were reconciled to him through the death of his Son, how much more, having been reconciled, shall we be saved through his life!" (Romans 5:10)

God did a further work of redemption on the Cross. (It is actually all one seamless packet.) He not only put on Jesus the penalty of our sin but He also nailed our sinful nature on the Cross with Him. When we receive Him as Savior, and lay down on the Cross the sinful, selfish side of our nature, He puts His own nature into us by giving us the Holy Spirit, and our spirit becomes *one* with His. By drawing from this new nature we can now live *naturally* by His ways if we choose to. God does not impose from the outside His high moral standards on us. He implants His nature in us, which behaves, and function in different ways than our old fleshly nature.

The life of the Spirit, received at salvation,

empowers us to live the life described in the teachings of Jesus. Everything behaves according to its nature. God solved the problem of sin not by giving us more commands to try harder and harder but by giving us His own nature. He exposes the weakness of our nature as we received it from birth and implants a new nature in us. It is natural for the old nature to behave sinfully. It is also natural for the new nature - since it is the nature of God - to behave morally and in a godly fashion. The secret is not to put pressure on the old nature but to replace it with His own life. What an amazing solution to the problem of sin!

God empowers us with His Spirit, not to exempt us from moral behavior, but to equip us for a higher moral behavior than the religionist. We achieve this not by self-righteous effort but by drawing continually from His life. Jesus said, *"Apart from Me you can do nothing"*. (John 15:5) So He does not expect us to do this *apart from* Him, but empowers us to do this *with* Him. *"I can do all things though Him who strengthens me."* (Phil. 4:13) We like to say to the Lord "I can't but you can!" Through the infilling of the Holy Spirit He empowers us to live by His way and through the Baptism in The Holy Spirit He empowers us to do His works.

"So now there is no condemnation for those who belong to Christ Jesus. And because you belong to him, the power of the life-giving Spirit has freed you from the power of sin that leads to death. The Law of Moses was unable to save us because of the weakness of our sinful nature. So God did what the law could not do. He sent his own Son in a body like the bodies we sinners have and in that body God declared an end to sin's control over us by giving his Son as a sacrifice for our sins. He did this so that the just requirement of the law

would be fully satisfied for us, who no longer follow our sinful nature but instead follow the Spirit." (Romans 8:1-4)

The above tells us that when the life of Christ comes into us His life releases us from the law of sin and death. When a plane takes off the laws of aero dynamics releases it from the pull of gravity. As long as the engines are running properly the plane will be able to go forward free from the pull of gravity. This is because the law of aerodynamics, released by the motors of the plane, is stronger than the pull of gravity.

Sin is stronger than human will power and our old nature no matter how educated, religious or morally refined it is. However, sin is not stronger than the life of the Spirit. When we have received the life of the Spirit - Christ in us - this New Life lifts us from the control of sin. As long as we choose to lean on Him and draw from His life, sin will have no more control over us. It is not a matter of trying harder - it is a matter of being filled with a new life and drawing from it.

"And I will give you a new heart, and I will put a new spirit in you. I will take out your stony, stubborn heart and give you a tender, responsive heart. And I will put my Spirit in you so that you will follow my decrees and be careful to obey my regulations." (Ez. 36-26-27)

The blood of Jesus releases us from sin's penalty and the life of the Spirit releases us from sin's power. This is God's solution for all the dysfunctional behavior of mankind. God's program for the moral reform of the world is to place His Spirit in us. Once we know this, it only remains for us to draw and rely on His Spirit even in the face of our weakness. *"But he said to me, 'My grace is sufficient for you, for my power is made perfect in weakness.' Therefore I will boast all the more gladly of my weaknesses, so that the power of Christ may rest upon me."* (2 Cor. 12:9)   The Holy Spirit - not religious effort- is the antidote for sin.

Life In The Kingdom Of God

When we are reconciled to God we are transferred from the darkness of sin and alienation from God into the bright light of His presence. The life of the Spirit empowers us to live in a new way. It empowers us to live a life of love and kindness. This life is lived only as we lean on, and become completely dependent upon, God our Father and the life He supplies. That is the way of the follower of Jesus. He realizes, that as long as he draws on the life of the Spirit, the ways of the Kingdom of God will manifest in his attitudes and behavior. He also realizes that, if he fails to draw from the life of the Spirit, his old ways will manifest. As long as we draw from the life of God and lean on His provision we cannot sin. As long as we fail to trust and lean on the life of God we will continue to sin.

Drawing from the life of the Spirit requires cooperation. It requires *the use of our will* - not to demand more of ourselves - *but to draw by faith* from the life of the Spirit. We consciously choose to lean on the life of God, lay down our own self-righteous efforts and depend on the life of the Spirit. We draw on the life of the Spirit to reproduce in us the fruit of the Spirit *"love, joy, peace, patience, kindness, goodness, gentleness faithfulness and self- control. Against such there is no law."* (Gal. 5:22-23) One who *walks* in the fruit of the Spirit needs no external behavior code because the fruit of the Spirit will also produce perfect behavior. This fruit comes not from the fruit of our natural life but from the presence of Christ who is in us by His Spirit.

We choose to put off our old patterns of behavior that are incompatible with the ways of the Kingdom of God. We draw from the life of the Spirit to produce His ways within us. We live by the ways of the Kingdom of God as explained by Jesus in His teachings. We choose to be poor in spirit i.e. totally dependent on God for everything. We choose to be meek not dominated by our own opinions and ways but yielding to the counsel and ways of God and His Word.

When we come to the Lord we are released from sin's power by the life of the Spirit. However, some of the old ways may still be present in our attitudes in our minds and in our emotions i.e. in the soul realm. Our spirits are saved and our minds and attitudes are undergoing transformation. We put off, in cooperation with the Holy Spirit, old ways and attitudes that are incompatible with God's ways. In this way we enter more fully the ways of Kingdom living.

When we reconnect with God we receive His own life and we are born again. This is *an instantaneous event* when we accept Jesus as our Lord and Savior. However, entering into the life to the Spirit *is a lifelong process* of bringing our lives and minds more completely under the control of the Spirit as we learn to rely more completely on His power and help.

Chapter IV

RELEASE FROM THE CONTROL & AGENDA OF THE SYSTEMS OF THE WORLD

There is a third level of the believer's liberation - liberation from the agenda and control of the world.

God liberates us not only from our guilt but also from destructive ways of living. He wants to give us a new set of goals and purposes that liberate us from the control of the values and measurements of this world. In ancient Egypt God emancipated the children of Israel from slavery to Egypt. Their lives and energies were forcefully spent under the dominion of Pharaoh and in advancing the goals and agendas of their Egyptian masters.

The blood of the Lamb of God opened up a way for them to leave Egypt. It brought them out of the oppressive dominion of Egypt and under the direct dominion and protection of the Lord. They were able to abandon slavery in Egypt for the adventure and high calling of following the Lord and His plans for them.

In a similar way the Blood of the Lamb of God, Jesus, emancipates us - if we follow Him - from the agenda of the world. When we are born again, reconciled to God and filled with His life, we receive an inheritance with Him. Part of our inheritance is to walk in the plans and purposes that he has prepared us for us. We are emancipated from the world to pursue the plans and purposes God has for our lives.

'For we are his workmanship, created in Christ Jesus for good works, which God prepared beforehand, that we should walk in them.' (Eph. 2:10)

"For he has rescued us from the dominion of darkness and brought us into the kingdom of the Son he loves," (Col 1:13)

God saves us, not only to take us to Heaven when we die, but for good works that He wants to bring forth through our lives here on earth.

Unfortunately a great section of believers continue to live by the values, measurement and ways of the world and never discover the adventure of following Jesus as Lord. Some even try to use their faith to coopt God to fulfill their plans rather than heed the call to release their plans to Him. Others try to adapt the morality of the Kingdom of God to suit the morality of the modern secular world.

Many churches emphasize the free gift of salvation and fail to emphasize the pursuit of the new life, lifestyle, values and plans that God has for us. Through faith in the finished work of God we receive salvation and become heirs of God. We then SEE the kingdom of God. Through obedience to the life of the Spirit we ENTER into the kingdom.

The world - especially at this time in history - walks to a set of values and measurements that are very different to the values and ways of the kingdom of God as taught by Jesus. It is vital that the believer breaks free of the world's mold to pursue a life in harmony with the ways of Jesus and the leading of His Spirit. When we walk to a higher standard of values than the world around us, and refuse to compromise with its values, we may be misunderstood and suffer injustice and persecution.

Though we walk to a higher standard there is no self-righteousness in our walk. We live this life not on the basis of personal superior ethical abilities but by realizing we are no better than anyone else. We are aware we can only live this life as we draw by faith from the new life principle Christ has place in our hearts - the Holy Spirit.

Receiving release from the world's agenda and control requires a DECISION to put the leading of the Spirit and the plan of God above any other choices, motivations and opinions of our own.

"And he died for all, that those who live might no longer live for themselves but for him who for their sake died and was raised." (2 Cor. 5:15)

In the early part of the letter to the Romans, Paul explains how the free grace of justification - based on the facts of Jesus' work - is received by faith as a gift. This is followed by the infilling with the life and power of the Spirit that emancipates us from sin's power and empowers to live in God's ways. Finally, here in the twelfth chapter of Romans, he pleads with us to take one more step to align our lives with God's purposes and plans. He asks us to give God our lives to live for the agenda of the Kingdom of God and not for the agenda of the world.

> *"I appeal to you therefore, brothers, by the mercies of God, to present your bodies as a living sacrifice, holy and acceptable to God, which is your spiritual worship. Do not be conformed to this world, but be transformed by the renewal of your mind, that by testing you may discern what is the will of God, what is good and acceptable and perfect."* (Romans 12:1-2)

Paul here expresses God's plan to the believers who have been redeemed that we now give ourselves over to God's plans and purposes for our lives.

This is the life of the disciple. This invitation is for the follower of Jesus. If anyone presents their lives to the Lord for His agenda and puts the direction of His Spirit and Word above their personal preference, their personal opinions and their old patterns, they will increasingly discover the life of the kingdom of God. It is what Jesus speaks about when He says, *"If any man would come after me, let him deny himself and take up his cross and follow me. For whoever would save his life (soul) will lose it; and whoever loses his life (soul) for my sake and the gospel's will save it. For what will it profit a man if he gains the whole world, and loses his own soul?"* (Mark 8:34-35)

The word 'life' (psuche) in this passage is a mistranslation. It should read 'soul' (mind, will, intellect and emotion). Jesus is saying that whoever wants to follow Him should be willing to surrender their preferences to God. Anyone who chooses to live for the purposes of God will lose some things in the short term but will receive far greater fulfillment in the long run. The pursuit of God's will is more fulfilling than the pursuit of mere personal ambition. We learn to subordinate our own preferences, goals and opinions for the purposes of God.

Jesus invites us to follow Him and become His disciple - to exchange our plans for His. This is a further voluntary response that every believer who is already 'saved' from sins penalty and power is challenged to make in response to the Lord's love. He challenges us to lay down our preferences to follow Him. He pleads with us to make ourselves totally available for His agenda setting aside our own ambitions.

"If anyone desires to come after Me, let him deny himself, and take up his cross, and follow Me. For whoever desires to save his life (soul) will lose it, but whoever loses his life for My sake will find it." (Matt. 16:24-25)

Our obedience does not add to what Jesus did on the Cross. Taking up OUR cross is simply surrendering our wills to God's purposes and putting the leading of the Spirit ahead of our own self-centered desires and ambitions.

This is not an excuse to 'drop out' of our natural responsibilities in life, to work, provide for our families and study with diligence and excellence. It is a call to place every aspect of our lives under the direction of the Lord. Our work, study and social lives are placed in the context of the bigger picture of living for God. An engineer, nurse, teacher, doctor, plumber who gives his energies to an evil regime lives a completely different life than one who places his talent, life and decisions at the disposal of the Lord.

The one who makes Jesus His Lord, constantly makes his life choices in the context of the question "What would you have me do Lord?" "Lord, show me where to go, what to do, what to be involved in, what not to be involved in."

This becomes a lifestyle of the surrendered believer until there is perfect harmony between His will and God's will. The dualism of two separate wills disappears and our will and God's eventually come into complete harmony.

It is important to note here that the Lord asks us to follow Him and to present our bodies as a living sacrifice for His good plans and purposes. He does not ask us to present our bodies to another person, a work, a denomination or movement. As we relate to Him He will connect us to others and will connect us to different groups, but our dedication is not primarily to them but to Him. Failure to recognize this distinction has sometimes caused people to devote themselves to institutions rather than to the Lord Himself. Wrongly focused dedication can cause the Lordship of Jesus and the leading of the Spirit to be diminished and usurped by men - even good men.

"But you, do not be called 'Rabbi'; for One is your Teacher, the Christ, and you are all brethren. Do not call anyone on earth your father; for One is your Father, He who is in heaven. And do not be called teachers; for One is your Teacher, the Christ. But he who is greatest among you shall be your servant." (Matt. 23:8)

The disciple - the one who presents His life to the Lord to live for Him - subordinates His own opinions and choices to the call and purposes of God. He loses his life (soul) and gains a far more wonderful one. He overcomes the agenda of the world, the measurements of the world and the entrapment of the world. As he responds more to the ways and directions of the Lord through His Spirit and His word, his mind is renewed, his will makes different choices, his attitudes change. The world's measurements cease to control him and he enters the life of the Kingdom of God. He not only *hears* the words of Jesus but also gives himself to live by them, relying on the Holy Spirit to *do* the works of Jesus.

"Therefore whoever hears these sayings of Mine, and does them, I will liken him to a wise man who built his house on the rock: and the rain descended, the floods came, and the winds blew and beat on that house; and it did not fall, for it was founded on the rock." (Matt. 7:24-25)

He loses fear of man or dread of the future. By the power of the Spirit, he can enjoy comfort and endure hardship. He knows that while there are difficulties, tribulations injustices and persecutions in the world, there is also abundant comfort in the Lord and that all things work together for His good.

"Blessed be the God and Father of our Lord Jesus Christ, the Father of mercies and God of all comfort, who comforts us in all our tribulation, that we may be able to comfort those who are in any trouble, with the comfort with which we ourselves are comforted by God. For as the sufferings of Christ abound in us, so our consolation also abounds through Christ." (2 Cor. 1:3-5)

The plan of God is for the Body of Christ to enter this third dimension of salvation becoming part of His team of reapers in the end-time harvest on the earth and to light up the world with His love and His truth.

Baptism In The Holy Spirit

When the believer surrenders his life and makes Himself available to the Lord's work of advancing His Kingdom and fulfilling the Great Commission - God has a second Blessing for him - the Baptism in the Holy Spirit. The Lord empowers him by His Spirit - if he asks Him - to do the ministry works of a disciple and proclaim the gospel accompanied by the miraculous. This empowerment of the Holy Spirit, which Jesus called "Baptism in The Holy Spirit" is available to all who give themselves to God's purposes, being aware of their complete inability to do Gods' work apart from the enabling power of The Holy Spirit.

'And he said to them, "Go into all the world and proclaim the gospel to the whole creation. Whoever believes and is baptized will be saved, but whoever does not believe will be condemned. And these signs will accompany those who believe: in my name: they will expel demons; they will speak in new tongues; they will pick up serpents with their hands; and if they drink any deadly poison, it will not hurt them; they will lay their hands on the sick, and they will recover.'" (Mk 16:15-18)

In the gospels we see that the disciples received the New Birth and *infilling* of the Holy Spirit on the day of the Resurrection but later, on the day of Pentecost, they received the *power* of the Holy Spirit *upon* them to do the works of Jesus. They hungered, yearned and waited for His endowment as they dedicated themselves to go into the world to proclaim the benefits of Jesus' work, in obedience to His words.

"And now I will send the Holy Spirit, just as my Father promised. But stay here in the city until the Holy

Spirit comes and fills you with power from heaven." (Luke 24:49)

"But you shall receive power when the Holy Spirit has come upon you; and you shall be witnesses to Me in Jerusalem, and in all Judea and Samaria, and to the end of the earth." (Acts 1:8)

Note the disciples had already received the Spirit *within* them. They were waiting for something more - a heavenly enduement of God's ability to do God's work. Tragically many believers today ignore this great endowment and are left doing God's work in natural energy and limited power. We need the great enduement to fulfill the Great Commission!

The surrendered believer can ask God to clothe Him with Power from on High. They then rely on the presence of Jesus and on the Power of the Holy Spirit to carry out the Great Commission.

Absolute Surrender & Total Dependence

The disciple loses his soul to find it. He receives not only salvation in his spirit but also in his soul. He develops the attitudes of Christ, walks in the ways of Christ, submits his opinions to the mind of Christ and participates in the work of God. His will is surrendered to the Lord and he walks in the childlike care of His heavenly Father

Since life in the kingdom of God is a life under the leadership of Jesus, in the care of the Heavenly Father, it is also a life of total *dependence.* We look to the Lord to direct our paths. We look to Him for our assignments and we depend on the power of His presence to enable us to walk in His ways, manifest His character and do His works of love.

It is a life of ABSOLUTE SURRENDER and TOTAL DEPENDENCE.

CHAPTER 5

SALVATION OF SPIRIT, SOUL & BODY

Our Amazing Inner Technology

Humanistic (Greek) philosophy defines man as a "soul in a body" but the Bible reveals a *completely different* understanding of man. Each one is a SPIRIT who has a SOUL and lives in a BODY. The humanistic understanding has robbed us of true understanding of who we really are and the incredible and unique capacities with which we are endowed.

What distinguishes us from animals is not the sophistication of our brains but the fact that we - unlike the animals - are spirits. We are spiritual beings with the capacity to relate to the physical world with our bodies and the spiritual world through our born again spirits. When we are reconciled with God through faith in the atoning sacrifice of Jesus our spirits are reconnected and come alive. The whole realm of communication with God, and the Kingdom of God, now becomes real to us.

As reconnected spirits we have the inner "technology" which enables us to communicate with God. This 'technology' is like a Wi-Fi modem within us that gives us the capacity to receive COMMUNICATION from God. We also have the capacity to receive spiritual LIFE from God, (1 Cor.

15:45, John 20:22) LOVE from God (Romans 5:5) and even to receive impartation of GOD'S OWN NATURE. (2 Peter 1:5.)

In examining the three aspects of salvation: salvation from sins' penalty, salvation from sin's power and salvation for God's purposes, we have noticed the tension between these three aspects of salvation.

- The SALVATION OF OUR SPIRITS from the penalty of sin is a gift to be received by faith.
- The salvation *from sin's power* is achieved by relying on the life of the Spirit to operate in us as our life principle and to set us free from the 'law of sin.' We refuse to return to self-righteousness and to draw from the old failing, self-life, but draw by faith, on the life of the Spirit to pursue God's ways.
- The SALVATION OF OUR SOUL is achieved as we surrender our ways to the ways of the Lord. The soul of man is his mind, will, intellect, attitudes and emotions. As we pursue the life and vision of the Kingdom of God and give ourselves for the Lord's purposes we are emancipated from the world and our souls are *progressively saved.*

"But we all, with unveiled face, beholding as in a mirror the glory of the Lord, are being transformed into the same image from glory to glory, just as by the Spirit of the Lord." (2 Cor. 3.18)

This brings to an end the old argument between the Calvinist and Arminians - between those who say that to receive salvation we need do nothing but receive, and those who say we must also put off the old ways and put on a new set of values of choices can now be solved. Both are right and both are wrong. Salvation of the spirit is a free gift to be simply received by faith, but salvation of the soul requires our choice and constant surrender to the ways of the Lord.

Both groups fail to see that the scriptures speak about the salvation of the spirit and the salvation of the soul in different ways. Traditional Christianity failed to notice this vital distinction in the scripture so the church became divided between those who emphasized behavior as a condition of acceptance and those who ignored behavior. One became permissive and the other became legalistic. The answer is that those who have received acceptance and the new life of the Spirit (salvation of spirit) are also called to pursue salvation of the soul. Salvation of the soul is the result of putting the mind of the Lord, (word of God) and the perfect will of the Lord above our own mind, will emotions and desires (soul).

The scriptures that speak about the cost of following the Lord address the issue of the salvation of the soul and our progressive entry into the kingdom of God, here on earth. The scriptures that talk about the free gift of remission from sin's penalty (being fully reconciled to God) apply to the salvation of our SPIRITS.

"As many as are being led by the Spirit of God are sons of God." (Romans 8:14)

"For the word of God is alive and active. Sharper than any double-edged sword, it penetrates even to dividing soul

and spirit, joints and marrow; it judges the thoughts and attitudes of the heart." (Hebrews 4:12)

"Whoever desires to come after Me, let him deny himself, and take up his cross, and follow Me. For whoever desires to save his life (soul) will lose it, but whoever loses his life (soul) for My sake and the gospel's will save it." (Mark 8:34-35)

To save our souls we lose them! We, according to Jesus, allow them to be completely made-over. We allow Him to give us a new set of values, a new set of goals, a new set of attitudes by which we guide our lives. We allow our lives to be led by our 'born-again' spirits rather that be dominated by our own will, intellect and emotions (soul).

Being led by the spirit rather than by the soul does not mean that we repress our emotions, or do not use or develop our minds, but we are *not controlled* by them. It simply means that we put the leadership of the Lord, through our born-again spirits, ahead of the pressure from our minds and bodies. When Jesus asks us to deny our souls to follow Him, He is neither being sadistic or masochistic. He is asking us to subordinate the preferences and opinions of the mind to the leadership of His Spirit so that we can enter into the destiny, which our Heavenly Father planned for us. To take up our cross to follow Jesus is not an invitation to any kind of self-hatred or masochism. It is simply God directing us to the abundant life He has for us. To return to His ways we have to abandon our own plans for self - realization so that He can direct us to the better things and ways He has for us.

"Trust in the Lord with all your heart, and lean not on your own understanding. In all your ways acknowledge Him, and He shall direct your paths." (Proverbs 3:5-6)

The whole aim of losing our soul is to learn to live in perfect harmony with our Heavenly Father and His more excellent ways. We seek to do nothing that is not in harmony with the Word, the Spirit and the ways of God. We do not run ahead of the Spirit with our own plans, ideas and opinions, but we subordinate everything to the Spirit and the Word of God.

In Gethsemane as Jesus faced the Cross, He said to His Father *"Not my will but Thine be done. My soul is sorrowful even to death. Nevertheless not my will but Thine be done."* He chose His Father's will ahead of His own preferences. He was keenly aware of the difference between what His soul (his mind, emotions and natural inclinations) wanted to do and what the Spirit of His Father was directing Him to do. He surrendered His soul to the direction and plan of His Father *and "became obedient unto death."* As a consequence He purchased our redemption and He Himself entered into an even greater glory and joy. Similarly He asks us to put the leadership of the spirit ahead of our preferences so that God's life, which has come into us, can come flowing through us.

"Let this mind be in you which was also in Christ Jesus, who, being in the form of God, did not consider it robbery to be equal with God, but made Himself of no reputation, taking the form of a bondservant, and coming in the likeness of men. And being found in appearance as a man, He humbled Himself and became obedient to the point of death, even the death of the cross. Therefore God also has

highly exalted Him and given Him the name which is above every name," (Philippians 2:5-9)

Renewing Our Minds With The Word

Our souls are further 'saved' by being renewed in the word and surrendering to the Spirit and the Word of God. In the renewing of our souls, the three main elements of the soul are involved - our wills, our intellects and our emotions.

Surrendering and choosing God's will, plans and ways save our wills. His will becomes ours. Receiving the word of God with meekness saves our intellects, and submitting to the timing and ways of God saves our emotions. We receive renewal of the intellectual part of our souls by renewing our minds with the Word of God. Jesus prayed we would be sanctified with the truth. To be sanctified does mean not that we become religious "Holy Joes" but that we are committed to God's plan and liberated from the world's agenda - by receiving and living by the truth.

"Sanctify them by Your truth. Your word is truth" (John 17:17).
" If you continue in my word, then are you my disciples indeed; and you shall know the truth, and the truth shall make you free." (John 8:31-32)

"Receive with meekness the engrafted word that is able to save your souls" (James 1:21)

We renew our minds from the programing of the world by constantly filling them with the Word of God and by meditating on Our Heavenly Father's words, His plans, His ways and His promises. The pressure of the opinions of man, the trends of the world, and the measurements of others lose their control.

The salvation of our souls is a life long process of renewing our minds in accordance with the Word, and subordinating our wills, thoughts and emotions to our Heavenly Father's plans. As we meditate on God's Word and especially on Jesus's words our minds are filled with the thoughts of Heaven and in this way they are renewed and made-over.

> *"Blessed is the man*
> *Who walks not in the counsel of the ungodly,*
> *Nor stands in the path of sinners,*
> *Nor sits in the seat of the scornful;*
> *But his delight is in the law of the Lord,*
> *And in His law he meditates day and night.*
> *He shall be like a tree*
> *Planted by the rivers of water,*
> *That brings forth its fruit in its season,*
> *Whose leaf also shall not wither;*
> *And whatever he does shall prosper."*
> (Psalm 1:1-3)

When we renew our minds we re-train them to live according to the new identity we have in Christ. This kind of mind renewal allows God's work in us to completely transform us. Most believers do not allow their minds to be renewed fully by the Word of God and because of this fail to discover and live out the potential of their new creation life. Paul yearns the *'we might know the things that have been freely given to us by God.'* (1 Cor. 2:12)

Salvation Of Our Bodies

As believers our bodies are 'kept' by God

from the curse prescribed in the law. *"May your whole spirit, soul and body be kept blameless at the coming of our Lord Jesus Christ."* (I Thess. 5:23) The Lord blesses our bodies and heals them.

"Bless the Lord, O my soul; And all that is within me, bless His holy name! Bless the Lord, O my soul, and forget not all His benefits: Who forgives all your iniquities, Who heals all your diseases, who redeems your life from destruction, Who crowns you with lovingkindness and tender mercies, who satisfies your mouth with good things, so that your youth is renewed like the eagle's." (Psalm 103:1-5)

The Lord made abundant provision for the blessing and healing of our bodies. Through the fact that He has placed our diseases on Jesus we live in a whole new realm of divine health. On the Cross, Jesus took our diseases and pains on Himself so that *"by His stripes we are healed."* (Isaiah 53:5; Matt. 8:17; 1 Peter. 2:24)

"But he was wounded for our transgressions, he was bruised for our iniquities: the chastisement of our peace was upon him; and with his stripes we are healed." (Isaiah 53:5)

In addition the overcoming Spirit of resurrection that comes into us at our new birth energizes and gives life to our bodies. The same power that blasted Jesus out of the Tomb victorious over all the sin and weakness of the Adam man now "quickens" and gives life to our individual mortal bodies.

"If the Spirit of Him who raised Jesus from the dead dwells in you, He who raised Christ from the dead will also give life to your mortal bodies through His Spirit who dwells in you." (Romans 8:11)

All believers should discover, rely on and take advantage of these great realities, and look to the Lord to keep, heal and give resurrection life to our bodies here on earth.

Our bodies are also affected by changes in our souls. As our souls put on the ways of the Kingdom of God and we develop a life of faith, love, joy and peace our bodies are also affected.

"Beloved, I wish above all things that you may **prosper** *and be in* **health***, even as your soul prospers." (3 John 1:2)*

As our souls prosper so do our bodies. Countless medical studies verify this reality and the effect of our emotions on our bodies through the endocrine system. They verify the healing power of forgiveness, joy, love, service etc. - the attitudes of the Kingdom of God taught by Jesus. The health of the body is dynamically connected to the health of our souls.

Scripture also encourages us to exercise stewardship over our bodies by moderate and wise eating, bodily exercise and avoiding drug abuse and immoral uses of our bodies. *"I discipline my body like an athlete, training it to do what it should."* (1 Cor. 9:27)

Though the Lord keeps, heals and gives life to our bodies they are not yet fully redeemed. They are still subject to decay since they are tied into the fallen condition of the creation, which is 'groaning' for redemption. As believers we long for the day when the creation will be fully redeemed, and our bodies also fully redeemed at the return of the Lord.

"For we know that the whole creation groans and

labors with birth pangs together until now. Not only that, but we also who have the first fruits of the Spirit, even we ourselves groan within ourselves, eagerly waiting for the adoption, the redemption of our body. For in hope we have been saved, but hope that is seen is not hope; for who hopes for what he already sees?" (Rom. 8:22-24)

The redemption and full salvation of the body is in the realm of hope. It is part of the salvation that Jesus will bring with Him at His return. *"So also Christ died once for all time as a sacrifice to take away the sins of many people. He will come again, not to deal with our sins, but to bring salvation to all who are eagerly waiting for him."* (Hebrews 9:28)

"But our citizenship is in heaven, and from it we await a Savior, the Lord Jesus Christ, who will transform our lowly body to be like his glorious body, by the power that enables him even to subject all things to himself. (Phil. 3:20-21)

- We can say that ***our spirits are saved*** by faith in the work of Jesus on the Cross
- ***Our souls are being saved*** as we yield to Him and surrender to His purposes.
- Our bodies ***will be fully saved*** at the return of the Lord

PRAYER TO RECEIVE SALVATION

Heavenly Father, I come to You just as I am. I acknowledge my sins and turn away from them. I believe from my heart, that on the Cross Your Son, Jesus took my blame, shame and atoned for these sins. I accept Your forgiveness and I in return forgive all others for whatever they have done against me. I give my entire self to You, Lord Jesus, and put it under Your protection. I ask You to come into my heart and make me a new creation. Take all bitterness, anger and selfishness out of my heart. Fill me with Your Spirit and replace my old sinful nature with a new and right spirit. Live in me and love through me. I promise to live your way and ask You to empower me by Your Holy Spirit to live it. I shall follow you every day of my life. *"Now Jesus, you live in me and I live in you. Amen"*

PRAYER OF SURRENDER

Lord I present myself to you to be your disciple and to pursue Your purposes for my life. I lay down my independent plans, opinions and ambitions, and yield myself to You. I lean on the life of Your Spirit to live a life free from sin's power. I formally present myself to You to live as an agent of Your, love, mercy, and truth on the earth.

Prayer To Receive Baptism In The Spirit

Dear Jesus, I give myself to You for Your purposes. I want my life to be used by You as an instrument of Your love, and of Your gospel to the world. I do not have the power for this. I ask you now to baptize me mightily with the Holy Spirit and with power. Holy Spirit come upon me with all Your gifts and graces. Give me a spirit of love and compassion, power and might, boldness and utterance, faith and humility, revelation and understanding. I receive you now from the hands of Jesus as my Enabler to live a life dedicated to You and to Your kingdom, and I will pray in tongues, as you give me the ability.

(Pray this prayer in an attitude of receptivity only if you have made a complete consecration of your life to the Lord. Prayer is not magic - it is the transaction of holy business with God through faith, which is released in words.)

(Note praying in tongues is not magic. To speak in English we move our vocal chords and tongues to make sounds. Praying in tongues is exactly the same. It is always under our control. We use our tongues and vocal chords to make sounds. However we give the Lord syllables, which we do not censor with our minds. As we give the Lord our syllables the Holy Spirit makes it a language to God that bypasses the mind and expresses the intents of the Spirit.)

PAUL & NUALA O'HIGGINS

Paul & Nuala O'Higgins are the directors of Reconciliation Outreach. They are natives of Ireland living in Stuart, Florida. They travel extensively in an international ministry of teaching, reconciliation, healing and evangelism. They spend several months of each year in Ireland.

Paul holds a doctorate in Biblical theology and Nuala is a graduate in education from the University of London. They are the authors of several books.

To order books contact: Reconciliation Outreach www.reconciliationoutreach.net
P.O. Box 2778, Stuart, Florida 34995
Tel. US. 772-283-6920
paulandnuala@comcast.net

Other Books By Paul & Nuala O'Higgins
- Christianity Without Religion
- Life Changing Prayer
- The Supernatural Habits
- The Four Great Covenants
- The Blessed Hope
- In Israel Today With Jesus
- Good News In Israel's Feasts
- Have You Received The Holy Spirit?
- New Testament Believers & The Law.
- Do This In Remembrance Of Me
- The Real Mary

Printed in Great Britain
by Amazon